ROOTED

MIRIAM DAMARIS MALDONADO

Translated from the Spanish by Walter Krochmal.

A Books&Smith Indie publication.

Rooted

All rights reserved © Miriam Damaris Maldonado.

Copyright 2022.

Published in the United States of America by Books&Smith Indie in collaboration with author Miriam Damaris Maldonado.

This is a work of poetry entirely from the imagination of its author. Similarities with people, places or situations are the product of chance.

It is forbidden by the governing laws of copyright to copy, distribute, or manufacture this work in any possible form, be it virtual or in print, by any means, past, current or future, in parts or as a whole, without previous written consent from its author.

Edited by Silvia Heller.

Author photo by Dianny Henriquez.

Formatting, Final editing, and cover design by Books&Smith Indie.

Translated by Walter Krochmal.

First edition 2022.

ISBN: 978-1-7368848-4-3

*To my experiences, the fruits I got from them:
Juniel Cotto and Damie Cotto.*

Acknowledgments:

I'm grateful for the music that caresses each parenthesis of life, poetry itself, and my life mentors: Josefina Navarro, Mayra Santos Febres, and Gabriela Baeza.

I thank:

my ink sisters, Vanessa Torres, Rossy Lima, and Erika Said, for listening to me and sharing wine nights and our history.

The *Colibrí Feminist Collective*—which has filled me with knowledge.

Rosaly, for the shared dreams, for believing in me and making me look good.

My colleague and sister Violeta.

Myr and Raquel Salas because they walk with me and teach me.

José Vélez, who teaches me how to live with strength (thank you, thank you, thank you.)

My father, who taught me to let go of fears and embrace my essence.

My children, Juniel and Damie Cotto, who have endured the absence and presence of my emotions, who have grown with me and been the engine to everything.

To everyone who's believed in me, thank you.

Foreword

True poetry, I have come to believe, does not busy itself with matters concerning the sophistication of language or the banal embellishment of its verses by way of the superfluous. A serious artist of the written word, the one we so aptly call 'the poet', entangles herself with something far beyond the often-found despair of language—its inadequacies, its finite luggage of responses. This 'something' we talk about lies in a realm exclusive to that chosen breed of humankind; and only they who have dove heart-first into the depths of that ocean of endless turmoil in search of beauty beyond reality can begin to grasp what (and how much) that 'elusive something' means to them.

Perhaps the most common trait of that mysterious thing is the fact that it comes in as many shapes and faces as each individual's imagination—or capacity for self-exploration (self-exploitation?)— will allow. For what else is poetry if not the quintessential test of transparency? [Necessarily for both writer and reader.] Where else can such beauty be found? For we must agree: the beauty pursued by poetry is not conventional, but all the opposite: it shatters the conventional in order to discover, uncover or build the sort of beauty that cannot only be admired but felt, that will not only awe but cut, not only wound, but heal...

Where, then, can such a thing be found if not within the self?

Language, whether modern or old, can only suffice in its purpose to become an efficient channel of expression if the poet has driven herself (the way Miriam has in this case) to attain the beauty savagely hidden behind pain and humiliation. Beauty as catharsis. Poetry as catalyst of such catharsis. For the pain portrayed in this collection of poems is not custom-made: it is a pain shared by millions of women—a sort of profound, soul-clenching pain that at times seems just unbearable. And yet, a poet like Miriam comes along and uses the might of language (not its excesses or vanity) to create a river stream, so beautifully crafted, so encompassing, so familiar and heart-reaching, it manages to drag all this pain along its banks and shed it away into the vast and plural sea of self-affirmation. In other words, the poet takes the mysterious thing poetry is made of and molds it into a palpable artifact of healing: this book.

Edgar Smith
October 10th, 2023.

ROOTED

Borinquen

In summoning your memory
a sliver of sea
has fled
from between my eyes.

Hell's Genesis

I was fine and did not know it,
fine not gorging on his anxieties
over discovering a good book
whose characters hold the reader
fast, taking on their form

I was fine
not casting out the anguish
and burning desire to be Lilith
eating Adam's each
and every son... alive

Then, though,
he intoxicated me in his temple
[white heat]
in the venomous misery
of his gaze, in his misogyny,
woven of fabricated feminism
in his letters, scattered,
as the hangover looms.

Status

I like to feel divorced,
to puke up the hackneyed coins
of barter and trade

I like to believe myself divorced,
to summon the hapless phoenix
that poured inside my belly
a pitcher full of lava

I like to think of myself as divorced
even when the hands on the clock
melt at six with the aroma
of just-served dinner

—flavorless and bland

I like to imagine myself divorced
(hold the goblet 'til I break it)
Perhaps even shushed,
bleeding,

or seeking
my shattered self

All I know is that I like
to dream myself divorced.

Ancestresses / Roots

Of sisterly ink

Ink overflows in my blood
which the wind howls
heavier than water

It has turned sour, untameable,
etched on skin
weathered by experiences bygone

It pours out 'til it shatters me
into tiny bits
scraps of childhood
on the village log pile

And I fly, sister,
light, free, become word,

verb, dry ink...

Alive in every heartbeat
in every letter
that calls our names.

Supplication

To my goddesses and she-demons

You dwell in every light beam
and shadow of my gait

You exist inside and out
of the universal womb

You begat my Orisha goddesses:
Yemayá, Ochun and Oya

My she-demons, too: Lilith, Saint
Martha and Pomba Gira

The ancestresses who cradled me
and those who forsook me
in an attempt to avoid themselves

You are all of them
in her and in me
in one single flesh
and in all energies

Grant me the strength to give
my universe berth as you gave it
to your daughters, that they might
lift the oceans

They found shared ground in Eden
and gorged to feed their own fruit

Give me the will to find my actions
enough, unbind guilt
and free me of mine

Heal, mother of mine, heal,
bearer of life and heiress of death,
of all our stories,
fill them with rites

Let us dance on the other side
of Eden and build a place
now hurtful, now loving

Our garden of delights
found within us in our now

Bring me back whole in every shard
shield me from the patriarchate

and what has been learned

Walk back every morsel
of the bad taste

May the lure of your fire nourish us
now and in our magic hour,

evergreen ones.

Collector

They called my grandmother
l*oose* in the village.

She corrected them:

"Collector of kisses"

Everyone in my family
is a collector,
so how could you not
understand her?

Me, a collector of farewells
She collected the feverish saliva
that gets entangled, the moist
kisses, the pecks
the forced ones, the after-a-weeping-
spell ones, the failed ones,
the wedding kisses…

I went my way, gathering moments
(in airports) made of extended

embraces that weave
themselves into your skin;

in restaurants with dim light
and awkward smiles, half-gazes
eyes brimming with ocean;

at wakes with coffee;

in villages with chicken broth
and not-to be-told stories,
on the last calendar day dressed
in juicy cuts of meat
in a miraculous girdle

I collected farewells in the kisses
that my great aunt, in her haste,
let vanish in her wake, for later.

Ori for Damaris

Ori,

to my blessed high spirit
for my days are shrinking
for my memories are shrinking
high spirit of the mangrove

Ori,

catch me on the corner
on the sidewalk or waiting
at the door

(which might be open?)

Conceal me in your light
and give me the freedom, Ori,
of an open seaport
ringing out like bowls
with the full, raving tide

a solid stardust blend,
ethereal

Light me up with great faith,
with great good fortune

A sharp-to-the second lure
for the wagging
tongues,
fo' painstaking saving
of your blessed sanity

Ori,

For letting biases go
for untangling fears and privilege
start yearning to be mortal.

Shake up my tale
of belonging to another
plant brown-sugar
wound-healing roots

Ori,

Fire, Air, Water, Earth, Sky, Stone,
Salt and Sea

Spirit and Matter
Remembrance...

We are

—for my blessed head.

Self-Portrait (Ancestresses)

I resemble her
but don't want to

yet neither do I want
to vacate myself
and exile myself
from my gestures

I resemble her
more than my grandmother
who stored *ashé*
in my strands of hair
and coconut oil,
untangling fears
and bad habits

I resemble her
stripped of privileges
storing seashells in my smile

as she told me, tooth for tooth,
about all the lovers she never had

I resemble her
who rebuffed the incense
who breathes in her gaze
who also hides the other

grandmother,
the gypsy with the cutting glance
broadish nose, slightly slut-sharp
nostrils holding the aroma of those
two grandmothers
with their necklaces which *Yemayá*
helps them bead,
love-stained apron
for errant granddaughters,
redolent of the sovereign olive
in the center of the dough,
pastel wrapped in a leaf
just because

Yes, I resemble her in every line
that I do not write, in the pauses,
shadows and silences,
as a daughter of violence

It is because she,
orphaned from me,
orphaned from the daughter
of the inheritance,
of the flavors and smells that dwell
on my lips

ajar

insists on forgetting recipes
spells and stories
where the nectars pool and turn
potion of balsam-pear

I resemble her lips
where my grandmothers
heal bit by bit.

Insomnia

Another

sleepless

night

drilling

my

mind

aimlessly.

Vouched-for / Trunks

She-body

Translated by Dr. Octavio Quintanilla

This she-body
all knowing
Explored
Exposed
Self-ritualized
Self-discovered
Empties itself in the fullness
of its own reflection

This she-body, recycled scar
Artifice of a system that consumes
That nourishes a withered smile
Fertile memory

This she-body, mine, just mine…
With horizons and traces of home
With tiny secrets and signs
Filled with bits of
coconut and mango
lodged between pores

This she-body,
map of my dread and my loves,
The forgotten ones
The ones I still remember

This she-body, mine,
in a smile in exile
and in ethereal manifest.

Witch

There are potions
that don't get swallowed

they're balms

Sometimes what heals the skin
does not enter the body

Some potions know you
and wait for you
'til you find the exact formula,

what was missing
or what was in excess

There are potions that no longer
hold secrets, that heal what's
deepest-cloaked

They shapeshift:
the hard and stubborn

There are witches who remake
their essence, their broom,
their myrrh and incense;

who change, fly high and glide,
knowing themselves witches

for all time.

Tender of Resignation

I resign from writing love poems:
the kind that choke your now
wrapping your waist in bare excuses

I will resign from the militant
practice of seeking out
some other me
to make me whole

I resign from withering
in an attempt
to submerge my patterns
in an orgy of thirsty,
housebroken wolves

I resign from the gall
to mute my ancestresses
rites and remedies strung together
at my core.

Ode to the Little Girl That I Never Was

In harmony,
you were raising the Eden
they stole from you

Beautiful near-faun of a lass,
lass of the reef,
lass of the castle turret
lasses all

island lass, archipelago lass,
who breaks away from you

They gave up on your childhood
which selfsame sprouted
in your belly
with the scorn of
"everything happens for a reason",
the sarcasm of
"each one comes with bread under
our arm"

Little lass of the waters,
who hid in your pigtails
the stories that as of today you roar

You gave yourself the treat
from the
street
of remaining a stranger
to the belly of violence

Now you dwell in yourself
a bellow hidden in the shadows
that peers out to embrace you

Blessed *tamboras* in your gait,
you raised life high
in your *plátano* thighs
charted a map of caresses
on your skin

The din of abandonment
by a mother

you're silenced like a bird's eye
in a music score

'til you birthed the melody and lyric
that shapeshift to nurture you.

The Wound Laid Bare

I want

to make peace with me,
to like me so much that it suffices,

in earnest, though
no amazement
no masks
so as to show them
with life spilling out at its whimsy,
no thought of pardoning or
pardoning with the wound laid bare;

I want to talk to life about life,
find myself in a sliver
of sea and not drown

Embrace myself there
where I sit sometimes
and curl up fully, all of me,
in my own arms

unguarded.

Sometimes Lady Poets Marry and Divorce...

"I was just another poem in her life," my ex-husband told the judge in the same courtroom where we swore upon the eternal flame

It wasn't like that, though. He was not just another poem, he was a great poem, un *poemazo, the* poem

I think he was right, half-hearted, unseen, gropingly, but with the selfsame certainty of being right

And what is *right?* As if there were an absolute definition

He had that, he had *right* on his side, and I had poetry

Assets were distributed thus: he got to be totally right and I got to keep all the poetry, that's what the judge suggested. Such a sensible judge!

When I fell in love with my ex, I changed from the inside out

New words sprang to life, the ones we all know: archaic, shopworn, on the shelf, but, as they reached my lips, they were new

I saw words peopling his neck, tossing around on his torso, walking on his lips and I'd kiss them to ensnare them and not forget them; yet my mind disconnected from my mouth and I would kiss him again and again, with words aplenty on his skin, his lips

That is where the conflicts began

Intense, he would call me, whenever I saw a word and wanted to tether it

to my mouth, my hands, my thighs
and hips; I never wrote them down,

I just fed on words and more words

I sewed them, hid them, wove them
together, but write them down,
never

I feared they might eye each other
prone on a sheet of paper and stop
blooming from his skin

I fed on beautiful, stealthy, crass,
outlandish, tender, sensuous words,
on all words

They were inside me, sometimes
roving my underarms and sliding
onto my hands, which then quivered

One day the word "heat" hid among
my fingers, and I rushed to moisten
my lips with my tongue

Serious mistake

There were more words there: you, bliss, I arrived, I have, love, you produce, me, now, I need

All those words began slipping through my fingers

The more I moistened my fingers, the more they mixed in my mouth...

You, bliss, I arrived, I have, love, you produce, me, now, need, heat

That's why when the police officer stopped me to explain that I ran a red light and asked me (in an authoritarian tone):

"Ma'am, could you pull your fingers out of your mouth and explain to me what is going on?"

I said to him:

"Love, I'm feeling hot
you make me blissful
I need you right now"

For that reason, Your Honor, this matter is closed: my husband read in the police report the words that lived on his lips.

Equinox / Flora

Green Handkerchief

I, too, tangled my shadows
in the patriarchy

I hid my belly, full of fears

I destroyed a muted, full-bodied
world to which I belong

I denied being the witch
of my own alchemy

I ran naked in iron buildings
I bundled my secrets in the fate
of my strands of hair
I made silence, my *compadre*
hesitated in the tenderness
of violence
planted thorns in me and my sisters

I built a temple of only the decent

draped myself with the guilt
of all that is uncertain

walked with Sodom
and Gomorrah under heel

I quaked, too, on seeing my death
calling myself a feminist
coming to life again

to being.

To Be

I am like all orphan daughters:
daughter of the ancestresses who
forgot me and forgot themselves

I am like all daughters of violence,
daughter of all those who did not
know that they had daughters,
forsaking themselves on their path
gathering skeletons to render as
poetry,
metaphors that snap
in the cracked bones
of the evergreens

I am a daughter of muted women,
the mother of those who bellow too
and upend their world,
their universal uterus in a vast
motherland that feeds
a *bohío* woven of dreams,
a refuge hidden

in the secrets of bedrooms concealed
in the half-light

I am that passing, ethereal daughter
where they all gather,
a mutual dance.

To the Gaucho

Unravel my desire to
imagine you without me
to make of your name
a *bohío* in the South

Shelter my motherland
with your taste of firewood
Dress your voice in that same sun
that my son
and your tango melt together.

Medias voces

I miss that man who roams
the isles of my catastrophes,
approaches [almost whispering]
and understands that time heals all,

who floats, sure that time and I do
not exist and this is as real as
the future, as dusk,
as the odd place
where we never dwelt

Truths weep for the silence
of what we know

We don't say so
lest another truth be torn apart,
lest yet another wound bleeds
and the ooze chokes on its purity

We go to church,
doubts have no place there

If not in writing,

then the Torah gets burned
you and I join a kilometers-long
procession where the signs,
the Tarot, the conch shells converge
and the incredulity of
an accurate present.

To My Lady Therapist

Did I tell you I wrote him a poem?

It has the word "to crush"

I don't recall clearly

What I do recall
is my wrinkled chest
those unseemly heart-flutters

vulnerability that leaves
your body brimming
with little sweets and memories

Did I tell you I saw him yesterday?

It was all confusion
the way it's always been

I don't know if his eyes
grazed my lips
or mine slashed our dreams.

I wrote a poem for him,
chock-full of wordsies,
using the diminutive,

which I already know
he doesn't like

I wrote him something
teeny weeny, almost pretty,

all brimming over
in my crushed little chest.

To Say No

I never knew how to say *No*

It was an issue

Hence the little yes-no slips of paper
made me nervous

How to say *No* to such
an innocent little slip of paper?

Do you want to be my girlfriend?

Well, yeah.

I always had a bad memory

I didn't know how to remember
decisions.

How to face *this*, *that*
or a little bit of *whatever other*?

That is why
the little yes-no slips of paper
were an issue

the young boyfriends
that make your hands sweat
and those who promise you
company on the city bus

The little slips of paper
asking you for a *Yes* or a *No*
romped in the desks of some
and others and almost all
those to whom I could not,
by accident
out of conviction
or because I forgot,
say no.

To Damie

The night of October 24th
the hurricane returned
a slice of me tearing off
my body

The hurricane lashed and lifted
timbers when they had already
announced calm on the news

The doctors, some Cubans,
said that the girl would be able to
wear a bikini

That girl was me

You wanted to be born in a hurry,
not asking for permission
knowing yourself a warrior

You wanted to be born
to be loved

to build a bridge
two blocks away
to clean my knees
and keep walking

You were a hurricane girl
That returned
when they already thought
you would not come.

Mariposas Caribeñas

I write of butterflies
crawling in the castle turrets
turning into black Taíno women
who wash their surnames
where Pilate atoned for his sins

All of them,
prostitute virgins with eyes threaded
for real
fake-pious beauties
crushed by the collective silence,
throttled by colonizer spittle
All of them,
caterpillars on the wing
their blood heavy with bilí,
mariners housed on Isla Nena
with the human waste and cancer
sheathed in wargames

I write of butterflies
defoliating heretics

in bonfires of Capitol marble
when its Yankee poetry
vomits promises

I write of butterflies
Aflame
They bite and scratch
turned to magma
They rebirth,
shattering a bouquet of ribs

I write of butterflies
that rescue drowsy *coquíes*
full-throated, hunched over
to the beat of the *bomba,*
the *plena* and freedom.

3:11 a.m.

At that hour
the dead cling fast
to the world of the living

They tell us secrets
they insist on ruminating
over life events

"Light a candle for me,"
they whisper
so as to follow the light

At that hour
you and I
(who are, at times, a *we*)
rip our odds to shreds

At that hour
tortured, we wreck a clock,

its hands exhausted
prudish, drowsy clock...

yet it does not stop

At that hour
you wake me from a dream
that I never had
drowning we cross the threshold
of the present
sending up prayers
skirting the edges of hell to see
if the future catches up to us
and startles us

"I'm staying over there,"
you say

at that moment when I meet you
over there,
we don't know if we'll be there

"The present is best,"
I say

"The future is best,"
you say

I strike up another light
to find us alive.

Sororo Echo

This voice I like
it awes me,
weaves me in
one coquí and another
in a nest of gatherings

This balm of a voice
strokes me gently

this healing voice
to a
gathering,
weaving errant paths and bridges,
coquís that awake and hop around,
a tiny nest that throttles
colonized throats

That caressed voice,
which dreams that we're together,
that no there is no distance
or semi-distance

it shortens them
and sets them to music

That voice that you deny is mine
and ours, It is the one Neruda
ordered to stay quiet

and all of us,
the women who bellow and echo,
that voice which unites us
without stopping us,

Ay sí, that embraces
and understands us,

that voice is a single voice
draped in tears
and in the joys of the holy elements

and in the prickling palms
of our hands
that gets cast off onto a canvas.

Ashes

I am that
which neither remains
nor returns

I am something
which, dissolved in it all,
is nowhere to be found.

Dulce María Loynaz

I give you back my submissive smile
your barefoot tongue
I give all back to you,
	all that I never had

The sun frozen on my waist,
bitching butterflies turned to dust
your lips, conquerors of my
colonized skin
the bonfire of an afternoon that
never took place
a morning exiled with no yearnings

I make you a gift of prejudices
overflow the shelves
and twenty-one bare pantries
a breakfast at six in the evening
and the fire's whisper in your watch

In the living room,
I char the memory

of your absence, present
with no traces of sperm,
three throw pillows placed perfectly
on the hips of Old San Juan
I give you back the ashes
with a letter from Uncle Sam.

Poetic Theory on Loves That Stick in the Throat

At times, the dissatisfaction proper to my gender stalks me

it is no stereotype, or maybe it is; however, it could be a scientific fact like those that caress your mind —"fact" as my lady boss would say (you know, the "white" one)

At times —and only at times— my yearning fills with unmet fears and expectations, those that almost touch the wind, that dance with an atheist Christ smoking a cigarette that heals your Utopian cancer in a Houston bar where everyone (and no one) knows anyone at night's end, which is to say the start of another day

At times it approaches, all hunched over, whispering into the ear: live, fly, feel, bite, cry, laugh... but don't you stop

and I open the door to a cage that blankets me with a time-clock punched from 8:00 to 4:30 and I go out for a while and return to the cage to rest

"One day I will abandon the cage," I tell myself, always, at 5:00 or maybe on the 25th hour of yesterday's dream, that's where I'll leave the future laid out and take away the fears from it, one by one, for fears are sensitive and I'm fond of them at this point that's how it will go, while a truck driver disguises himself as Nietzsche and unbinds turns of the page never told in writing

Until he transports poetic theories and dataless bases that foretell a system of loves that stick in the throat.

Miriam Damaris Maldonado (Puerto Rico) is an award-winning poet and active promoter of cultural events in Houston, TX. Miriam is one of the founders/members of the movement *Colectivo Feminista Colibrí*. She is also an essayist, narrator, dancer and activist, who participates in and coordinates literary festivals.

She just published her first book of poetry *Enraizada* (Spanish, 2022, Valparaíso.)

She has studies in Human Behavior, Gender, and Diversity. She is currently studying Creative Writing at the *Universidad del Sagrado Corazón* in Puerto Rico. She also serves the community as a Social Worker and as a member of the *Colectivo de Grupos Puertorriqueños*.

Miriam Damaris is currently working as project manager with the Puerto Rican Literature Project.

Table of contents:

Pages:

15 / Borinquen
16 / Hell's Genesis
17/ Status
21/ Of sisterly ink
23 / Supplication
26 / Collector
28 / Ori for Damaris
31 / Self-portrait
34 / Insomnia
37 / She-body
39 / Witch
41/ Tender of resignation
42 / Ode to the little
girl that I never was
45 / The wound laid bare
46 / Sometimes lady poets marry
and divorce
53 / Green handkerchief
55 / To be
57 / To the Gaucho
58 / Medias voces

60 / To my lady therapist
62 / To say no
64 / To Damie
66 / Mariposas caribeñas
68 / 3:11 a.m.
71 / Sororo echo
74 / Ashes
75 / Dulce María Loynaz
77 / Poetic theory on loves that stick in the throat

Other poetry books from Books&Smith:

Viento del este / Wind from the East

Luisa Navarro

Voz propia / Voice of our own

Edgar Smith

Poems 2 Her

Steven Wise

Metáfora de lo indecible / Metaphors of things unsaid

Elsa Batista

www.booksandsmith.com

www.ingramcontent.com/pod-product-compliance
Lightning Source LLC
Chambersburg PA
CBHW030301030426
42336CB00009B/477